WELCOME TO THE FARM
Plow and Ripper

Samantha Bell

Published in the United States of America
by Cherry Lake Publishing
Ann Arbor, Michigan
www.cherrylakepublishing.com

Content Adviser: Gary Powell, Weed Science Research Technician,
Michigan State University
Reading Adviser: Marla Conn MS, Ed., Literacy specialist, Read-Ability, Inc.
Photo Credits: © New Holland Agriculture, cover, 1, 2, 6;
© nevio/Shutterstock, 4; © bbbb/Shutterstock, 8; © Samantha Bell, 10;
© Design Pics Inc / Alamy Stock Photo, 12; © Bonnie Henderson, 14;
© Suzanne Tucker/Shutterstock, 16; © oticki/Shutterstock, 18;
© rsooll/Shutterstock, 20

Library of Congress Cataloging-in-Publication Data
Names: Bell, Samantha, author. | Bell, Samantha. Welcome to the farm.
Title: Plow and ripper / Samantha Bell.
Description: Ann Arbor : Cherry Lake Publishing, [2016] | Series: Welcome to
    the farm | Includes bibliographical references and index.
Identifiers: LCCN 2015047228| ISBN 9781634710367 (hardcover) |
    ISBN 9781634711357 (pdf) | ISBN 9781634712347 (pbk.) |
    ISBN 9781634713337 (ebook)
Subjects: LCSH: Plows—Juvenile literature. | Agricultural
    machinery—Juvenile literature.
Classification: LCC S683 .B38 2016 | DDC 631.3/7—dc23
LC record available at http://lccn.loc.gov/2015047228

Cherry Lake Publishing would like to acknowledge the work of the Partnership
for 21st Century Skills. Please visit www.p21.org for more information.

Printed in the United States of America
Corporate Graphics

Table of Contents

4

Getting Ready to Plant

The farmer wants to plant a crop. First he or she tills the soil.

What things would you find in the soil?

Farmers till with **plows** and **rippers**. A tractor pulls them.

Disk Plows

There are different types of plows. A disk plow has a round shape. It turns the soil over.

It pushes weeds under the soil.

Breaking the Soil

Big tractors pull big plows. A moldboard plow turns over the soil.

A ripper cuts into the soil, too.
It can go very deep.

The ripper makes the soil loose.
Roots grow better in loose soil.

Where does the driver sit?

Planting Seeds

The soil is ready. The farmer plants the seeds.

What things do plants need to grow?

The new crop will be growing soon!

Find Out More

Dorling Kindersley. *John Deere: Big Book of Tractors*. New York: DK Publishing, 2007.

History Channel—Modern Marvels: Farm Plows Kick Up Dirt
http://www.history.com/shows/modern-marvels/videos/farm-plows-kick-up-dirt#
Watch a short video about the history of the plow.

Glossary

crop (KRAPH) a plant grown as food
plows (PLOUZ) farm machines used to cut, lift up, and turn over soil
rippers (RIP-urz) farm machines used to cut into the soil
roots (ROOTS) the underground parts of plants that take in water and materials that keep the plant healthy
tills (TILZ) prepares the soil for planting

Home and School Connection

Use this list of words from the book to help your child become a better reader. Word games and writing activities can help beginning readers reinforce literacy skills.

a	farmer	moldboard	rippers	too
and	farmers	need	roots	tractor
are	find	new	round	tractors
be	first	of	seeds	turns
better	getting	or	shape	types
big	go	over	she	under
breaking	grow	plant	sit	very
can	growing	planting	soil	wants
crop	has	plants	soon	weeds
cuts	he	plow	the	what
deep	in	plows	them	where
different	into	pull	there	will
disk	is	pulls	things	with
do	it	pushes	till	would
does	loose	ready	tills	you
driver	makes	ripper	to	

Index

About the Author

Samantha Bell is a children's book writer, illustrator, teacher, and mom of four busy kids. Her articles, short stories, and poems have been published online and in print.